The 10 Be's of Positivity
10 Steps To A More Positive Way of Living

by Lynette Anneslia Turner

Published by Marble House Editions
96-09 66ᵗʰ Avenue (Suite 1D)
Rego Park, NY 11374

Library of Congress Cataloguing-in-Publication Data
Lynette Anneslia Turner, Positivoligist™

The 10 Be's of Positivity© <u>10 Steps To A More Positive Way of Living</u>

Summary: A self-help book that offers an uncomplicated method for improving one's life.

ISBN 978-0-9786745-5-7

Library of Congress Catalog Card Number 007926154
Printed in China

This book is dedicated to my parents, Anneslia and Herbert Turner, and my siblings, David, Gregory, Michael, and Karen, who always embrace my positive attitude, accept me for who I am, and encourage me to be true to my authentic self. I love you dearly.

Praise for *The 10 Be's of Positivity*

"This is a practical book, filled with wisdom which can easily be applied to one's daily life. The changes it can coach you into creating will help you to enhance the quality of your life and heal your emotional wounds."

-**Bernie Siegel, MD** and author of *365 Prescriptions for the Soul* and *Love, Magic and Mud Pies.* www.berniesiegelmd.com

"What a perfect book! *The 10 Be's of Positivity* is wonderful, brief, and my kind of book. The 10 Be's are easy to remember and will help every reader live life to the fullest and be happy."

-**Dr. Robert Muller,** Co-founder of the University of Peace. Dr. Muller has served as Assistant Secretary General of the United Nations, and is author of several books, including *Most of All They Taught Me Happiness.* www.robertmuller.org

"Lynette Turner's book the *10 Be's of Positivity* is a must-read for anyone wishing to understand and expand their well being in life. Lynette's comprehension of happiness is matched by her living each of the 10 Be's in her own life. Be Happy Now! Buy this extraordinary and illuminating book and reach out to B all you can B!"

- **Lionel Ketchian**, Author of *Food for Thought*. Mr. Ketchian is also the founder of The Happiness Club. www.happinessclub.com

"Lynette Turner spreads sunshine wherever she goes. The ten steps to positive living she offers in her heart-centered book will help you reach for the joy behind the clouds of even the darkest day."

- **Robert Moss,** author of *Conscious Dreaming.*
www.mossdreams.com.

"Do something positive for yourself; buy and read this excellent book. When you apply Lynette's 10 Be's of Positivity to your life, your true self will emerge, enabling you to live the life you were meant to live and to fully become the person you were meant to be."

-**Trudy Griswold**, spiritual success coach and author of *How To Talk With Your Angels.*
www.angelspeake.com.

Acknowledgements

Thank you to my colleagues at AMS Planning & Research for enduring my never-ending upbeat attitude, especially co-worker and editor Pat Durner; members of the Fairfield, Connecticut Happiness Club, especially founder Lionel Ketchian and members Don Barnett and Sharon Bornstein; Aaron Bryant, for his encouragement of my writing and his extraordinary editing skills, Kim Rich for her editing expertise and sense of humor, my best friend Lilla for always being there; Allen Sullivan for inspiring me to keep my independent streak by way of example, my dear friend Kashka; all of the Angelspeake™ courageous, crazy 8's, including mentors Trudy Griswold and Barbara Mark; manuscript readers and friends, Monica Piquet, Susan Carollo, Jayne Fletcher, Marla McGrail, Gloria Amendola, Dr. Michael Palmer, and Bobby Marini; Dave Ross, graphic artist extraordinaire, Jennifer S. Wilkov, CFP of ESP Press for her publishing consulting assistance; Elizabeth Uhlig of Marble House Editions for her publishing expertise and for publishing my book; Rick Frost for his unconditional love and support, and to each of you who are in search of a more positive existence.

Contents

"This will be a wonderful day, in each and every conceivable way."

- Lynette Anneslia Turner

Introduction

The *10 Be's of Positivity* provides a smorgasbord of choices that remind you to make the most of life's journey. You need not implement all the suggestions at once. Rather, think of the 10 Be's as options on a menu, and you can select whatever tempts your pallet. Your tastes might change over time and you may well shift your focus every so often. That's fine. Sometimes you might want a small morsel and other times a five-course meal.

This is an interactive book. Results require action. The 10 Be's are meant to stimulate you intellectually, emotionally and spiritually, and propel you into action. Following the narrative in each chapter, you are given a question to consider, a recommended action plan and an affirmation to help you along the way. In addition, consider the colors associated with each chapter as tools to help your action materialize. Visualize the colors suggested as you go about manifesting your desires. Colors have powers of their own and when envisioned, they can help bring a desired goal to reality and actualization. Remember, the restaurant is always open. Savor your choices, and *bon appétit!*

Attitude is also an important contributor to your overall well-being, and having a positive attitude is a primary ingredient for happiness. When you are in a positive state of mind you have the ability to address any situation. This simple formula will lead you down the path of achieving success, however you define it. If you visualize what you want and believe you are worthy of having it, everything will be within your reach. Anything you visualize and imagine can come to be. At its core, the 10 Be's of Positivity is about the power of the Law of Attraction. If your intention is to implement the 10 Be's into your life, then focus on *that,* and not on what you have *not* achieved. There is no need to struggle through the 10 Be's process. Life is meant to be an experience of ease and abundance. Change your attitude and you will change your reality.

I start each day by reminding myself, "This will be a wonderful day, in each and every conceivable way." In the words of the late philosopher Joseph

Campbell, "Follow your bliss." BLISS. **B**elieve **L**ife **I**s **S**omething **S**pecial, because it is ... and so are you. Enjoy the 10 Be's!

Sending Light, Peace & Happiness ~ Lynette Anneslia Turner

Embracing the Peace Within

Meditate • Write it Down • Live with Laughter

To prepare for the journey recommended in this book, I will suggest a few steps you can take to put yourself in the best frame of mind. You may have already incorporated these activities into your life, and if so, congratulations. Consider these suggestions "courtesy reminders" or activities that remind you of how you can stay focused on your intention. In doing so, you invite clarity into your life, and with clarity as a focal point, you can chart your own course.

A peaceful disposition awards many opportunities that you would not otherwise receive. When you are at peace, you are more apt to be happy, motivated and grounded. One way to achieve this is through meditation. Meditation is appreciated by many as a way to turn your thoughts inward. Meditation is defined in the dictionary as a practice to "keep the mind in a state of contemplation." If you are new to meditation, I encourage you to explore it. If you currently meditate, I encourage you to continue.

A few tips to help your **meditation:** Remember, it takes time to become good at anything. Be gentle with yourself. Through effort you will see and feel results, and with continued practice, you might find yourself thinking more clearly and being more patient with other people in your life. This will come about as the result of a committed effort. Meditation is about finding the stillness within you and allowing yourself to stay in a state of quiet thoughtfulness. Thoughts in your mind, however, might dart about like busy bees in a hive. When and if a rush of thoughts enters your mind, acknowledge it, but then let it go. Focus on your breath; let your attention move to the ebb and flow of your breathing. Start with a count of four. Inhale in for four counts, hold for four, and exhale for four. This is a good exercise to do anytime you wish to feel relaxed. You can play soft, calming music if it relaxes you. If you like candles, focusing your attention on the flickering flame can also help you reach a place of mental calm and peace. You can also meditate with your eyes closed if you find this most comforting. Spend a few minutes a day doing this and as time passes, you might increase your meditation to a time period that feels most comfortable to you.

My second recommendation is to keep a **journal.**
Writing down your thoughts, impressions, dreams,
and life experiences is a cleansing and expressive
experience. I have been keeping journals since
I was a teenager, and when I look back at what
I recorded, I realize how much I have benefited
from this practice. My journal entries include
poems, observations, and descriptions of what
was happening in my life. I have dream journals
and manifestation notebooks in which I record
in detail various things I want to manifest, such
as a particular job or a relationship with specific
qualities. Choose a journal that appeals to you. Buy
a blank notebook, which can be a simple leaflet,
booklet or a diary journal you find at a bookstore.
I like to buy a plain journal and decorate it myself.
I draw pictures, put favorite phrases on it and use
markers and crayons to adorn it. Artistry is not
my strong suit, but that doesn't matter. You want
to make it your own special book, so do whatever
you like to create a book you feel connected to.
Then…pick up a pen and write. Write down what
happened during your day, questions you are
pondering, or a dream you had. Whatever comes to
you, write without judgment. There are no wrong
entries. I recommend writing something *each day,*

even if the entry is short. Health research reports are now revealing that writing can help reduce ailments. People with asthma, for example, have improved lung function and others with stressful medical conditions have shown improvement as a result of journaling. Writing can be cathartic or it can serve as a pathway to releasing undesired conditions. I find it inspiring that journaling is good for your health. If something is bothering you, you release it from your mind when writing, which can also mean releasing if from your physical body, since tension can find a home in the body. Writing helps clear your mind and can help you to outline and solve problems. On several occasions, the act of writing out a challenging situation has revealed some possible solutions to me.

You should write down happy experiences as well as challenges, and if you like to draw, you can create images of your thoughts and memories. Writing is a freeing and worthwhile experience. I encourage you to try it.

Finally, **laugh each day.** Laughter soothes the soul, exercises every muscle in your body, radiates positive energy out into the universe, and just plain feels good. Studies on the power of laughter claim that laughing can stimulate the immune system and reduce stress. To quote comedian Milton Berle, "Laughter is an instant vacation," and I couldn't agree more. When you laugh, you are caught up in the moment. Your concerns take a back seat and you engage the mind, body and soul in this wonderful expression of joy. No matter what our day-to-day challenges are, we can all find something to grin about, smile about, or laugh about. Take 60 seconds a day and LAUGH!

After you've meditated, written down some thoughts that chronicle your existence, and have taken a moment to laugh, let's move forward to explore the 10 Be's of Positivity.

Thoughts on the Power of Color

Color plays an important role in the exercises suggested in this book. Therefore, I'd like to share with you why I include color as a part of the 10 Be's journey. Color relates to the power of positive visualization and taking action to receive results. In my work with dreams, I have learned that our dreams can come alive and work for us if we respect and honor them. This requires some activity in relation to the messages dreams bring. For example, if you have dreams about being in good shape, which show you exercising or eating right, you are receiving a message that indeed reaching this goal is possible. With this premise in mind, at the end of each chapter I offer a question to ponder, an action to take, a color to visualize associated with each topic, and an affirmation to help you keep on track.

While most of these areas are self-explanatory, I'd like to take a moment and share some thoughts in more detail about color and how it can be a powerful tool in your lives.

Color has played a significant role in enhancing a sense of well being and providing a means for healing in my life and in the lives of several people I know. I sometimes wear specific-color clothing, depending on my mood or the issue I'm addressing that day. I wear red if I'm making a presentation and want to grab the audience's attention or make a passionate appeal, and blue if I want to remain calm. If I visualize myself bathing in a stream of blue light, a sense of peace soon follows.

The power of color has been evident for many years and several great minds have explored its potential:

- The well-respected philosopher, Aristotle, linked colors with the four elements: water, fire, earth and air.
- Scientist Sir Isaac Newton's general color theory was accepted in the 17th and 18th centuries. Newton had the distinction of establishing the modern study of optics (the behavior of light).
- Hippocrates, a Greek physician born in 460 BCE, is considered the founder of medicine. He believed that sickness had a physical and rational explanation and that the body should be treated as a whole. He used color in his work with medicine and gave credence to the idea that different colors could have different therapeutic effects.
- Johannes Wolfgang von Goethe, an 18th century scientist, novelist, theorist and painter, wrote Theory of Colours, which offered some of the earliest descriptions of light and some ideas about color and what we can learn from working with these elements.
- Swiss psychiatrist Carl Jung's study of the human

psyche is legendary. He explored the mind by investigating religion, dreams, philosophy, mythology and art. He encouraged his patients to explore the power of different colors in their paintings, believing it would help them express the unconscious part of the psyche.

Colors affect each of us differently. The colors I suggest at the end of each chapter strike a positive chord with me and might do the same for you. If you don't feel connected with the color listed, replace it with a color that does resonate. What colors do you like and feel drawn to? As you reflect on the topic of each chapter, see what colors appear. You might discover which colors have value for you and how they make you feel. Comforted? Focused? Confident? Work with the colors as you further develop your ability to integrate the 10 Be's into your life.

Chapter One

Be Honest

Dictionary Description: Fair and just; free of deceit and untruthfulness; sincere

<u>*Positivity Thought*</u>*:*

Honesty as policy is powerful indeed. All that is required is that you truly believe, that you'll grow as a person and blessings will expand, when you have the gift of honesty, in front of you at hand.

Being honest, especially with yourself, can be a difficult exercise. You may sometimes be dishonest with yourself about issues that are challenging, avoiding them because it's easier not to take responsibility for your circumstances.

If you are unhappy about any area of your life, be it work, personal relationships or your own health, and you don't address your unhappiness, you aren't being honest with yourself, and dishonesty doesn't allow for growth.

How many people do you know who are unhappy with their jobs? You may be one of them. Do you often make excuses, telling yourself that you can't find another job because your skills are limited, or you'll never find a job that pays as much as the one you have? But what about the price you pay for getting up every day and spending time in a place you don't like? The stress of an unhappy work situation can cause irritability, and even sickness. What's worse, you might pass this energy along to your loved ones. Stress is not good for your physical or emotional well-being.

If you are interested in expanding your skill set but don't have the time or money, consider starting small. Your local community center or YMCA might have some free or inexpensive classes in your areas of interest. Take one class and see if it inspires you to take further action. Local communities sometimes offer grants that can make it affordable to take classes. If time is an issue, take a course over the Internet. These classes allow you to set your own schedule. Go for it! Life is short and we'd do well to make the most of every moment.

What's the payoff with being honest with yourself about your job situation? In order for things to change in the future you have to be honest now. Set a clear intention about what you want. Visualize the situation you want to have, release it to the universe and watch the magic happen. Step by step, your attention to detail can make a difference.

Are you happy in your personal relationships? Do you take time to nurture those connections? Hopefully you give your relationships the time and attention they need to grow and become stronger. Maybe you've outgrown a partnership and you're staying with a person because you're afraid of being alone, or don't think you deserve anything better. Erase that thought from your mind. You deserve to be happy and to be in relationships in which you are not only the nurturer, but are being nurtured.

And yes, it is better to be alone then to be in a relationship that does not bring you joy. Being alone can help you learn to appreciate your own company. This can be especially refreshing if you've been in a relationship with someone who told you that you were responsible for his or her happiness. You're not, of course, but you can start to believe you are if repeatedly told so. No one can *make* anyone else happy.

If you are alone, but would rather not be, trust that when the time is right, that other person will appear. In the meantime, understand that flying solo can be a gift to yourself when you learn to love and appreciate "you."

This is not always an easy place to be. Wishing you were in a fulfilling partnership while you are not in one will not make it so. But trusting that you are deserving of spending time with someone with whom you are truly connected, and being willing to go it alone until that person appears, is one of the most honest, fulfilling steps you will ever take. By spending that time with yourself and learning to embrace who you are, the experience of sharing your time with another will be that much fuller. A person who is honest with him/herself has the capacity to then be honest with others.

When you think of your personal health, what words or images come to mind? Do you think, "I'm fit, I have healthy eating habits, and I take time out of my busy schedule for myself?" Or do you think, "I'm overweight, I eat too much fast food on the run, and the last time I had time to myself I was coming out of the birth canal?" I don't need to tell you which one of these scenarios you want to be chanting. If you are a mother, wife, daughter, husband, father, son, employer or employee, boyfriend, girlfriend, or friend, to some degree you are taking care of someone else. You cannot do this well if you don't take care of yourself, eat right, exercise, or are a workaholic. You have to be honest about your needs AND TAKE TIME FOR YOURSELF!

What might that mean for you? A walk in the woods twice a week? A bubble bath on the weekends? A babysitter on a Tuesday night so you can go to a movie? A gardening class at your local community center? Whatever it takes to help you feel connected and appreciative of yourself, do it.

My personal weakness is sugar, so this is where I tend to over indulge. I know it's not good for me, really has no redeeming qualities, at least for my body, which tells me so when I overdo it. I'm not uninformed. I understand that too much sugar plays havoc with the body's chemistry. It can help lead to all sorts of ailments such as heart disease and hypoglycemia. But in my weakest moments I pretend I don't know these things or that they don't matter. I'm not being honest with myself.

Now I'm learning to stop whenever I crave sugar and ask myself what is really going on. Am I bored? Tired? In relaxation mode at the end of a long day? I'm usually one of these, but mistake it for craving sugar.

When I take the time to take stock of the situation and identify what's going on, I can steer myself in a more productive direction. It has taken me a long time to get to this point and I don't always succeed. At least now I can identify what's really happening to me and strive to react sensibly.

And remember that it's not mandatory or necessary for you to handle these issues on your own. If you need professional help, get it. Don't be afraid or unsure about getting support. If you feel you need guidance with challenging life issues, then you probably do. Doctors, health practitioners, clergy and self-help groups all serve an important purpose. They provide you with the tools to be healthier, feel better and to move your life in the direction that best serves you.

Be committed to yourself. Be committed to being honest. If one of the reasons you're not happy is that you're caring for everybody else, these other parties need to know that you intend to take a step back. You don't have to be mean-spirited or harsh to these "energy vampires," but you can ask your neighbor to give you some warning before dropping her kids off unannounced for you to babysit and you can stop postponing your vacation because you have too much to do at work. You'll always have too much to do at work, so it's in your best interest to start trying to do a bit more "life balancing." Start by being your own best friend and true to yourself. You are the person who is best qualified to take care of you.

Be - Honest
Question: Am I acknowledging those elements of my life that I am content with and those that need further attention?

Action: Make a list of areas of importance in your life, such as work, family, personal relationships, health, etc. Now ask yourself to what degree are you happy in each of these areas. If you have any discontent, put in writing the changes you would like to see and determine what steps you will take to facilitate these. Next, set a realistic timetable for this project. Visualize yourself happy on the other end of the situation. Small steps are fine, but make a firm decision to take action.

Color Association: Visualize **Red** - the color red is associated with the physical body, being grounded, stillness and courage.

Affirmation: I am honest with others and myself about how I feel. My well-being is important enough to me that I will make the necessary effort to take care of myself.

Notes/Thoughts:

_____

_____

_____

_____

_____

_____

_____

_____

_____

_____

_____

_____

_____

Chapter Two
Be You

Dictionary Description: The person, or person, addressed

<u>*Positivity Thought*</u>:

No one is quite like you, no one's as unique, no one sounds as you do when you act and when you speak. So be proud of who you are and cherish all you have to bring, for what you have to offer is a very amazing thing.

That sounds like a no-brainer, doesn't it? "Be You." But it's amazing to me how many people aren't really being their authentic selves. They are being who everyone else wants and expects them to be: their family, friends, lovers, co-workers and boss. How can you be accepted? Loved? Climb the corporate ladder? Perhaps by molding yourself into several different personae to please other people?

It's time to stop trying to live up to other people's expectations. Remove the work mask or home mask or whatever shield you are wearing and reveal the real you. I suggest this for several reasons. First, trying to be all these other things to and for other people is exhausting. Second, you miss out – as do the people you encounter – on the wonderful treat of knowing the real you. You are different from every other person out there. You owe it to yourself to explore and share who you really are. In the end, you will be appreciated far more.

Since we are multifaceted, the wonderful thing about revealing your true self is that you won't be boring! You won't disappoint others by showing them who you are. You'll be a shining example of what others can aspire to be. A person who is proud to speak their mind, wear whatever they like and sing out loud and off key if it pleases them.

One way that I express myself is by decorating my office space in a way that makes me feel comfortable. I put affirmations on the wall, burn candles often, and have a dream catcher hanging from my window. I don't expect anyone else in the office to follow me, but I sure enjoy what I've done to my workspace. Because I spend a lot of time there, I decided to make the area as comfortable and as "me" as possible. I wonder if this is why my office is one of the areas on the floor in which people like to come and take a mini-break? They sit down on the couch and chill out for a moment or two, and I always welcome their company.

Be you and enjoy the rewards you will reap as a result. Be you, because in reality there's no one else you can truly be. Be you, because until you are your authentic self, you won't have the wherewithal to focus on the core of your being and determine what your true purpose is in this life. Be you, because you deserve to feel the pure exhilaration of what being "your true spirit" will bring. Finding your authentic self might not be a smooth journey, but it will be an enlightening one. Know that in the end you will be grounded, uplifted, and energized. Be you. Go for it!

Be - You

Question: Am I genuinely revealing the "real me" to the world?

Action: Take the time to think about the way in which you interact with others. If you can pinpoint situations in which you pretend to be someone you're not, vow to be your *real self* the next time the situation arises and follow through with that intention. You'll know when you are pretending to be someone you're not. You'll feel it in the pit of your stomach; you'll hear that voice in your head reminding you. If you catch yourself in the middle of this scenario, acknowledge it. This will help you be your true self next time around.

Write your own personal mission statement. It can be just one paragraph or a whole page, and should address the following points: your life mission, the principles you stand for and what actions you are taking (or would like to take) in order to manifest what you've outlined in your mission statement. If you're not on your mission, what is it you'd like to be doing?

Color Association: Visualize **Orange** - the color orange is associated with movement, assimilation of new ideas, change, desire and emotions.

Affirmation: I am committed to being my true self and sharing the real me with the world.

Notes/Thoughts:

_____

_____

_____

_____

_____

_____

_____

_____

_____

_____

_____

_____

_____

_____

Chapter Three
Be Open-Minded

Dictionary Description: Open to new ideas

Positivity Thought:

To be open-minded will bring such rewards. Gifts will materialize; the world will be yours. Joys not imagined will surely appear, if you're open-minded, your path will be clear.

As we get older, we generally become more set in our ways. I suggest practicing active open-mindedness. It's a far more exciting way to live life.

How about reading a book written on a topic unfamiliar to you? Go see a movie that you wouldn't ordinarily consider because you're drawn to a particular topic (musicals, westerns, romantic comedies, action movies, etc.). Wear red when you usually only wear darker colors. Being receptive to other ways of thinking will open your mind, broaden your perspective and give you a new outlook on life. It will allow you to look at yourself or situations with an alternative viewpoint. You don't have to do anything astronomical, like throw out all your biographies and buy only science fiction, but something small will do. Try reading a science fiction novel, and afterward you might be surprised by how you are affected by reading it. Who knew how much fun it would be to escape to a vividly depicted world of make-believe?

Your imagination is limitless. Let it fly and don't be afraid of the blessings that open-mindedness can bring. Have you found that you are sometimes reluctant to be open-minded because it threatens your feelings of safety? When you are in control you feel safe. Being open-minded requires loosening the reins on the safety net a bit. When you feel safe you don't have to deal with the unknown or change. But what is to be gained by not stretching your thoughts, not embracing a wider vision? It can be invigorating to consider someone else's point of view just as you hope others would consider yours.

One of my favorite exercises is to imagine myself in someone else's position, perhaps see their point of view on politics, spiritual matters, or personal/professional relationships. This doesn't mean abandoning what I believe, just imagining what the situation looks like through someone else's eyes. When I let go of my ego and my desire to be right, I really do have a completely different experience. This gives me a broader view of the world and those who live in it with me. I am then an understanding person who can respect and appreciate other people's viewpoints.

A while ago, a friend asked me to go with her to see an animated film. I was resistant and said I didn't really like animation. Ever since I saw Walt Disney's *Bambi* as a child, I decided that no other animated film could make me laugh, cry and feel hope the way *Bambi* did. Why would I spend time and money on something I probably wouldn't enjoy? But I said I would go anyway, if only to be in my friend's company. Much to my delight, it was a wonderful movie. They've done a lot with animation since I was a child and that, combined with a great story line, made for an enjoyable experience. This is a small example of how being flexible and having an open mind can lead to a memorable experience. You don't know what you'll discover until you allow yourself to be open to new adventure.

One way to explore this style of functioning is to remind yourself of how much *you* appreciate it when people consider your point of view. Vow to return the good practice when the opportunity arises. If the idea is still not entirely appealing, just think of it as a chance to have fun. It most certainly can be an enjoyable experiment and an enlightening one too. You might find yourself in the midst of some very intriguing "ah-ha" moments.

The world we live in is rich in many ways. We have the option of regimenting ourselves to set rituals and a specific way of doing and seeing things. We all embrace comfort, but comfort and joy come in many forms if we're open to the possibilities.

Be - Open-Minded

Question: Am I being as open-minded and as flexible as I can be in order to embrace new experiences?

Action: Pick one new activity that you wouldn't ordinarily consider and dive into the experience wholeheartedly. Track your experiences by journaling and refer to your writings on a regular basis to see how you're doing.

Color Association: Visualize **Yellow** - the color yellow is associated with personal power, authority, energy, self-control, warmth, laughter and transformation.

Affirmation: I am an open-minded person, who accepts change as a way to experience a new perspective. I am open to embracing all the new joy that it will bring me.

Notes/Thoughts:

_____

_____

_____

_____

_____

_____

_____

_____

_____

_____

_____

_____

Chapter Four
Be Loving

Dictionary Description: Affectionate, warm attachment

Positivity Thought:

*To be loving is a great gift that all of us should try.
A feeling so magnificent it cannot be denied.
So love others as you love yourself and
your energy will shine.
For peace and hope and kindness are indeed
what you will find.*

Who would not appreciate being loving, loved, and lovable? The ability to be lovable and loved by those close to you offers many rewards. Woman or man, young or old, to be loved is something that most of us long for, and why wouldn't we? When someone else cares for us, it feels good. It can boost our self-esteem, provide us with someone else to focus on, and give us something to smile about. Being loved is rewarding.

How does one describe a lovable person? People who are kind and generous, unconditional, non-judgmental and have a positive attitude tend to be lovable. You want to be around them. They have an inviting energy you want to absorb. When you are loving, you radiate an energy that makes you attractive to others.

Being loving is a tremendous way to live your life. You might demonstrate a loving attitude toward your partner or family members, toward your co-workers and acquaintances, to your pet or with complete strangers. If you adopt a policy of being loving and you live it, your life will never be the same.

People who are loving are like a breath of fresh air.

Being loving sometimes means addressing others' needs and desires as well as your own. It means unconditionally having an open heart.

The first step in the world of love is to love yourself. Appreciate and focus on all the good you have to offer. See good in yourself every day. This is the essence of love. If you are loving to those around you, you are off to a good start, but your world will become so much richer once you do the same for yourself. You deserve it, so why not make a commitment to acknowledge that you are worthy of self-love and the love of others?

I celebrate the importance of loving myself in many ways. I place affirmations all around my house -- on walls, mirrors, inside my bathroom cabinet. When I see them, I feel inspired to share this outlook with others, both in word and deed. Some of these affirmations include "Dreaming Required," "Release All Attachment to Results," Joseph Campbell's, "Follow Your Bliss", and Eleanor Roosevelt's, "No One Can Make You Feel Inferior Without Your Consent." When I am reminded of these messages, I feel like a more loving person.

What can you do to embrace the loving person who resides inside of you?

Be – Loving

Question: Do I love myself?

Action: Every morning, without fail, stand in front of the mirror, look yourself in the eye and say, "I love you." If you already love yourself, delight in this exercise. If you don't feel like you love yourself, this exercise will help you. After you say, "I love you" add "because..." and one thing you love about yourself. I love you *because you are a kind person*, or I love you *because you are a good provider*, or I love you *because you are a hard worker*. The more you do this, the easier it will become. You are worthy of being loved, lovable and loving.

Color Association: Visualize **Pink** - the color pink is associated with love and compassion.

Affirmation: I love myself for the person that I am and all the good I have to offer. I am loved, lovable and loving.

Notes/Thoughts:

_____

_____

_____

_____

_____

_____

_____

_____

_____

_____

_____

_____

_____

_____

Chapter Five
Be A Good Listener

Dictionary Description: Capable, making an effort to hear; heeds/take notice of

<u>*Positivity Thought:*</u>

Being a good listener has its own rewards, for when you take the time to do so your attention leans towards being in the moment and showing that you care. What better way to be a friend and with others share?

Oh, what a joy it is to sit with a friend or family member and know that they are truly listening. They aren't interrupting you, offering a different opinion, or answering their cell phone while you talk. But how often does this happen?

Being a good listener is a learned skill. Not everyone is born with the ability to listen well. Are you an attentive listener or an active one? An attentive listener is someone who lets the speaker talk uninterrupted and does not offer verbal feedback in any way while he/she is talking. They are attentive, but not vocally responding.

An active listener may nod, offer feedback, or ask questions during the course of listening. Both types of listening are productive and can play a role in effective communicating. Which one do you practice? The one you choose to use depends upon the needs of the speaker, and it's fine to ask them what they need.

As someone is talking to you, are you forming opinions? Are you deciding whether you agree with what they are saying before they are finished? When someone is talking, the best gift you can give is to listen with an open mind and allow them to express what they are thinking or feeling.

If you are an attentive listener, appreciate the ability to help in silence. If you are an active listener, breaks in the conversation and the speaker's body language will provide clues as to when it's appropriate to interact.

Parents and children can find it difficult to listen to each other. Adults sometimes think that because they are older and presumably wiser, they know better. We need to give children the same respect we'd like them to give us, and listen to what they have to say. By listening, we set a good example.

Keep in mind that you can also listen with your body, for body language can be just as telling as words. Maintain eye contact, and keep your arms, shoulders and chest open. This lets the speaker know that you are paying attention.

Good communication is a win/win situation. One of the best indicators of love and respect is being a good listener.

I work a lot with dreams, both my own and other people's. I try to help people learn the tools they can use to interpret their own dreams. Listening to others describe their dreams can require a fair amount of quiet time while the person explains the scenes and responds to specific questions I have asked. I might be tempted to jump in and offer an opinion about what I'm hearing, but I've learned to give the dreamer sufficient time to tell their story without interruptions. This might not happen if I were to fill in the blanks for them. A time comes for me to share my impressions, instincts and reflections, but I do a far greater service by encouraging the speaker to make his or her own discoveries. Be a good listener and everyone benefits.

Be - A Good Listener

Question: Am I a good listener? Do I listen fully to the speaker or am I forming opinions as they speak? Am I interrupting or making the speaker's issues about me?

Action: The next time you are engaged in a conversation, make a conscious effort to be completely connected with the other person. Listen fully and communicate your intent to do so with your attentiveness and your body language.

Color Association: Visualize **Light Blue** - the

color blue is associated with communication, creative expression through speech, truth, wisdom, gentleness and kindness.

Affirmation: I am a respectful listener, listening with every part of my being and connecting with the speaker on every level.

Notes/Thoughts:

_____

_____

_____

_____

_____

_____

_____

_____

_____

_____

_____

_____

_____

Chapter Six
Be Grateful

Dictionary Description: Thankful feeling or showing gratitude/pleasant

Positivity Thought:

The habit of gratitude is something divine. Your life vision will blossom and all will be fine. For to embrace being grateful will nourish your soul, and untold fortune is sure to unfold.

No matter what obstacles you are dealing with, you can always find something to be grateful for. I truly believe, and I say this by way of experience, that things could always be worse. Are you unhappy because you have a small house, a used car and few friends? If so, consider being grateful because you own a house. Some people might never be in a position to do so. They move in with relatives, live in homeless shelters and many of the less fortunate must live on the street.

Do you long for a new car? You can have one one day, with diligent planning and saving, but for now bear in mind that some individuals have no means of convenient transport. They go from place to place using public transportation. And some people are even unable to do that, and must walk to get wherever they need to go.

Do you feel lonely, wishing you were more outgoing and had more friends? As a starting point, first consider yourself your own friend and rejoice in your very existence. When I moved to a new town 4,000 miles away from my home, knowing no one, I was alone, but determined not to be lonely. As a poet, I sought out poetry readings to attend where I could be among people who shared my same interest. Eventually, I found the courage to stand up and share my words. I volunteered at a retirement home in my neighborhood. And now, even though I am busy with many activities, I volunteer at a food bank. You can always find shelters, retirement homes, libraries and the like that are eager for volunteers. You will feel appreciated when you help others and again, it will help you count your own blessings. Helping others offers you the opportunity to meet new people, and sharing activities can help you feel as if you are a part of a community.

We have all heard the maxim, "The more you give, the more you receive." Through my own experience, I believe this to be true. When you are grateful for what you already have, more comes to you. This is the law of attraction. Your thoughts are energy and you will attract more to be grateful for if you focus on and appreciate that which you already have.

If you truly feel like you have nothing to be grateful for, try this exercise. All you need is a piece of paper and a pen. You woke up this morning or you would not be reading this. Be thankful for that. Is it sunny outside today? Be grateful if you appreciate heat. Is it raining? Be happy for the grass. Do you have a job, even if it's not your dream job? Do you have a pet? If so, you have something to be grateful for. Jot it down and start your day with that vision of thanks. You'll find that the best way to welcome each day is with gratitude. This is a particularly helpful exercise when you have a challenging day ahead of you because it forces you to focus on positive aspects of your life. More than once, working to identify gratitude by using a journal has helped me jumpstart my day and put life in a positive and compassionate perspective.

Here are a few entries from my own gratitude journal. You'll see that some of the entries reflect life's simple pleasures, while others appear grander. All came to me exactly when they needed to, and helped keep me grounded, appreciative and… grateful. *I am grateful for rain, I am grateful for laughter, I am grateful for light and love, I am grateful for whatever experiences I will have today, I am grateful for my meditation room, I am grateful for sleep, I am grateful for the songs that the Angels send and for the power of music, I am grateful for the peacefulness of light, I am grateful for family and friends, I am grateful that I am a Lightworker.* And the list could go on and on, given that I've been keeping a gratitude journal for years. The messages might repeat themselves, but they are always wonderfully powerful. Something to be grateful for always awaits you.

I like to appreciate silly little things that one might consider annoying and find the gem of gratefulness in the experience. The other day I was rearranging some items on my desk and I knocked over a big container of paperclips. They didn't just fall in one place, but all over the floor. I had two choices—to be irritated by the interruption, or to decide I needed a little break. I chose the latter and I just started laughing. I found myself feeling grateful — that I had paperclips and that I was physically capable of sitting on the floor and picking them up. For two minutes I took a break from being an adult and I was a kid crawling around on all fours on the floor.

Be - Grateful

Question: Am I as grateful as I should be today for what I have? Am I acknowledging my blessings?

Action: When you awaken tomorrow, note one thing you are grateful for and reflect on it throughout the day. Notice how you feel by the end of the day as a result of this exercise.

Color Association: Visualize **dark blue** - the color blue is associated with insight, imagination, concentration and peace of mind.

Affirmation: I am a fortunate being and soul. I am grateful for all that I have in my life.

Notes/Thoughts:

_____

_____

_____

_____

_____

_____

_____

_____

_____

_____

_____

_____

_____

Chapter Seven
Be Spiritual

Dictionary Description: Of the spirit or soul, as contrasted with bodily or worldly; religious; divine; inspired

<u>Positivity Thought</u>:

To acknowledge forms of spirit makes life's journey complete. It is a place of solitude where we can all retreat. For when we look to spirit to help us find the way, each day's experience has something to say.

Let's talk *spirituality*. I use this word to mean a connection to *spirit* and not necessarily to a specific religion. Spirituality, I feel, is in the eye of the beholder. For one person, being spiritual means being connected to a religion. For another, it may mean walking in the woods and communing with nature.

I consider myself a spiritualist. I believe in God and respect all organized religions, but don't adhere to any one of them in particular. I believe in a power higher than myself. I think that we are all on paths of learning, and our beliefs are linked to our paths as part of our individual process of growth.

As you continue your life's journey, you will want to decide whether or not you need to clarify a particular religious or spiritual belief. Explore, read, learn and share ideas, and in the end, select the path that works for you.

Consider that your journey might be fuller if you explore a spiritual path. You might find comfort in believing that you are not alone. I believe I am an old soul; I've been here before and I remember many past lives. I intend to keep coming back until I get it right. I believe in guardian angels and

I know they are helping me with different areas of my life. While I don't think my belief system is for everyone, I have found it to be both effective and comforting. Explore your own beliefs, embrace them and enjoy the peace of mind and guidance that comes from having a sense of spirit in your life.

If you already practice an organized religion or spiritual path, be it Jewish, Catholic, Protestant, Buddhist, a spiritualist, or the like, I imagine you gain something rewarding through your connection. If you are hesitant to accept any kind of a spiritual path, I encourage you to take a moment, sit in silence and ask yourself why. Is it because you've had hard times in the past and when you called on God, you were not answered? Is it because you believe that if you can't see, hear, smell or touch something, then it can't be real? People frequently don't have a concrete answer—they just don't believe that a higher power exists to guide and comfort them.

I think that identifying with a particular religion or spiritual belief provides for a great opportunity to feel grounded, knowing you have a source of guidance and comfort. You have nothing to lose by opening yourself up and asking yourself what you might gain by having some kind of spiritual energy in your life.

Because we are all so different, our spiritual practices will vary considerably depending on point of view, attitude, and how we get into a "spiritual comfort zone." One of the practices I have adopted is to create an altar. This can be a small area on top of your bureau, a special table set up in an area of a room, or an entire room set aside for meditation and contemplation. I have a spare bedroom, which is also my meditation room. It has a long, low table I have fashioned into an altar. This is where I sit on pillows on the floor and meditate, pray, sing, ask questions of my angels, and do long distance Reiki sessions. It is a place from which I derive comfort.

An altar can have anything you choose on it. On mine I have a copy of the Bible, statues of angels, fairy and tarot cards, pictures of my family, an ivory Alaskan mask (a gift from my best friend), printouts of affirmations, a chime, incense, stones from a local beach, my meditation and manifestation lists, and lots of candles.

Your altar should feel like a sanctuary, calm and peaceful. It is a place to come home to, where you feel as if you are at one with yourself.

I encourage you to explore a variety of practices and see what works for you. If you are able to assume a state of mind in which you truly believe that your existence is a gift, you will feel blessed indeed. Your faith can help you make it through a tough situation and fully appreciate a joyous one. You already are blessed. Now explore a way to celebrate that.

Be - Spiritual

Question: Have I taken the time to find a spiritual path that can play a role in my life?

Action: Take the time to explore a spiritual connection that will bring ongoing peace into your life. You have the power to decide what this action will be.

Color Association: Visualize **Violet** - the color violet is associated with spiritual will, divine wisdom, selfless service and perception beyond time and space.

Affirmation: I am a spiritual being who is practicing a spiritual way of life that brings me peace, love and guidance.

Notes/Thoughts:

_____

_____

_____

_____

_____

_____

_____

_____

_____

_____

_____

_____

_____

_____

_____

Chapter Eight
Be Positive

Dictionary Description: Explicit; definite/convinced, confident or overconfident in an opinion/in agreement; affirmative/optimistic

<u>*Positivity Thought*</u>:

Be positive of the power you have to manifest change,
To see a light–filled future, to pave the path your way.

That nothing is impossible, no mountain
you can't climb,

Be positive of your power and your
inner light will shine.

Be positive that you are here for a reason and you have a purpose in life. You are a worthwhile contributor to the world you live in. Be happy, because being unhappy is draining on many levels. It steals vital energy from your physical, emotional, mental and spiritual makeup. Be positive about your worth, because one simple smile from you can make a difference, not only to your loved ones, but also to complete strangers. Don't underestimate the power of a smile and its ability to make someone else's day.

Not too long ago I spontaneously decided to try a little experiment. I was seated on the airplane in an aisle seat. I smiled at each and every person who passed by me and I was curious to see if they would smile back. Without exception each person whose eye I caught smiled back at me - every single person. Now what could be cooler than that? It's simple, free, and for a moment, the immediate environment was a little brighter and felt good. That's what I call Life. And who knows, maybe some of those people passed a smile on to someone else.

Find contentment in the simple things and you will have a positive existence. Money, for example, doesn't guarantee a positive existence, nor will fancy cars and the most expensive fashions. That's not to say these items can't bring comfort and some amount of ease. But they won't if you're not already a person with a positive attitude.

One by-product of being a positive person is that living with an optimistic attitude can bring you happiness. What makes you happy, or what do you think *would* make you happy? Many people long to have a positive attitude but have decided that life is so difficult they really don't deserve to feel positive. They don't realize that it doesn't take a master plan to have a positive attitude and live a happier life. It simply requires that you have a change of attitude and the desire to live each day from a positive point of view. It sounds simple and it is. Look at all the challenges in your life as opportunities for learning. Trust that a greater power will be with you as you live your life. One of the most important things you can do for yourself, for your family, for your friends, for the universe, is to decide a have a positive attitude and be a happy person. Charge forward with faith and perseverance.

Be - Positive

Question: Am I as positive as I want to be at this very moment?

Action: Make a list of all the things that you can look at with a positive attitude. Post the list where you will see it often and let it serve as a reminder.

Color Association: Visualize **Gold** - the color gold is associated with illumination.

Affirmation: I make the decision today to live my life with a positive attitude.

Notes/Thoughts:

_____

_____

_____

_____

_____

_____

_____

_____

_____

_____

_____

_____

_____

_____

_____

Chapter Nine
Be Forgiving

Dictionary Description: Showing forgiveness: inclined or ready to forgive

<u>*Positivity Thought*</u>*:*

*Find a place within your heart to forgive
the people in your life;
anyone you think has harmed you or
brought forth any strife.
For once you can forgive yourself and
everyone around you,
the light and love and joy you'll feel will
no doubt astound you.*

The power to forgive. How many of you have ever been unhappy because you are focused on what someone else did to you? Have you allowed your feelings to be hurt? It is no fun to hear an unjust comment from a partner, a coworker taking credit for work you did, your brother taking your sister's side in an argument instead of yours. You want to forgive them but you don't know if you can. In some families, there are members who haven't spoken to each other in years because one or the other can't forgive each other.

No one else can actually hurt your feelings. Each of us can decide how we are going to interpret another person's actions, taking them personally, or not. If you remember that a person's actions have nothing to do with you and everything to do with them, you'll have nothing to forgive because you will never feel that you have been victimized. And if you are able to practice living in the moment, forgiving might come more easily to you because you are living here and now and not in the past.

Dr. Robert Muller, who served as Assistant Secretary General of the United Nations and co-founder of the University of Peace, said, "To forgive is the highest, most beautiful form of love. In return, you will receive untold peace and happiness." How true. When you don't hold resentment or unkind thoughts about others, you free up your energy to generate feelings of love, and that's what your existence is about. Dr. Muller's poem sums it up quite nicely.

Decide to forgive

For resentment is negative

Resentment is poisonous

Resentment diminishes and devours the self.

Be the first to forgive

To smile and take the first step

And you will see happiness bloom

on the face of your human brother or sister

Be always the first

Do not wait for others to forgive

For by forgiving you become the master of fate

The fashioner of life

A doer of miracles

To forgive is the highest most beautiful form of love

In return you will receive

Untold peace and happiness

If I find myself thinking and/or feeling as if someone should forgive me, I remind myself that no matter what the other person did, they were doing the best they could, being the best person they knew how to be at the moment. I believe that each of our paths is exactly where we are meant to be. There is always room to learn from mistakes and the opportunity to continue to move forward on our journey. So work to forgive those you feel have harmed you. Treat everyone as you would like to be treated. This is a good attitude to have in all circumstances. Can you imagine what the world would be like if everyone did that? It would be full of kind, generous, non-judgmental people. So forgive your brother, your former business partner, the neighbor who plays his music just a little too loud. Life is relatively short. Let's spend it celebrating the experiences and people we encounter. Life will be fuller for it.

Be - Forgiving

Question: Am I being as forgiving a person as I want to be at this very moment?

Action: Make a list of the people who you would like to forgive you, or who you feel mistreated you and you would appreciate them seeking forgiveness from you. Write a letter to that person expressing your desire. You can choose whether or not to send the letter (the intent will induce results even if you do not mail the letter). Surround the letter with the color green. By doing so you infuse it with compassion and understanding. See the recipient receiving and accepting the letter. Let go of any tension you might be holding. Release. You have done your part. Now let the universe do the rest.

Color Association: Visualize **Green** - the color green is associated with compassion, understanding, peace, openness and contentment.

Affirmation: I make the decision today to live my life as a forgiving person.

Notes/Thoughts:

_____

_____

_____

_____

_____

_____

_____

_____

_____

_____

_____

_____

Chapter Ten
Be Present - In The Moment

Dictionary Description: The fact or condition of being present; one that is present.

<u>*Positivity Thought*</u>*:*

People who are present and in the moment have something figured out. They realize wholeheartedly what respect is about; for if being in the moment were your companion, how soon you'd realize that having this awareness in the big picture awards you the prize.

There is something deliciously calming about living in the moment. Do you find yourself in such a rush that you don't experience the journey? Are you impatient with your kids, co-workers, the elderly lady in line at the grocery store, and every other driver who is going too fast or too slow?

When did we become so impatient? Studies show that viewers want the images on the movie screen to change every four seconds in order to keep their attention. The ability to move around on the Internet keeps getting faster and faster, keeping up with our thirst for speed.

We equate moving slowly or methodically with wasting time. We have things to do and people to see. But once we are doing those things and seeing those people, we often rush so that we can move on and charge through the next task.

Your body, mind, and soul deserve your undivided attention. Practice living in the moment and having patience will start to come naturally. As a matter of course, when you appreciate the *now*, your levels of tolerance and appreciation grow.

Try eating dinner while sitting down, not standing at the kitchen counter with the TV on, while reading the paper or going through the mail. Eat without any other distractions. Savor the taste of the food in your mouth. Delight in its aroma. When you're at a four-way stop sign and you have stopped at the same time as the other driver, let him or her go first instead of gunning the gas to go through the intersection. What difference does it make in the big scheme of things? Zip, zero ... so slow down. See what's around you. Try being single-mindedly involved in whatever you are doing. This is living in the moment.

I have always been a patient person and prone to appreciating whatever is happening. I don't finish other people's sentences. I don't care if the slow-moving woman with the baby stroller halts traffic on the sidewalk and I really don't mind long lines. Moving slowly is truly a gift because appreciating what's happening gives you the opportunity to absorb what's going on around you. Rejoice in the experience of taking the time to observe whatever is happening. Enjoy that sensation; embrace it, be patient.

I contend that if you can be present/in the moment, you will be able to achieve all the other nine Be's of Positivity offered in this book. Being in the moment will lay the foundation for the rest.

Be Present – In the Moment

Question: Do I currently live in the moment?

Action: The next time a challenging event takes place in your life, ask yourself what effect it has had on you and appreciate that the experience happened for a reason. There is always something profound you can learn from any occurrence. Take the opportunity to do so in the moment of it happening, and your life will be richer for it.

Color Association: Visualize the color **white**, which is associated with truth and sincerity.

Affirmation: I am a positive thinker and a positive doer. I live in the moment consistently every day.

Notes/Thoughts:

_____

_____

_____

_____

_____

_____

_____

_____

_____

_____

_____

_____

_____

_____

Live the 10 Be's of Positivity©

To all of you out there, I encourage you to be **open-minded** as you move through life. **Be grateful** for what you have and **honest** in your assessment of your life. Be flexible with yourself and other people. **Be a good listener** to others and you will find the same in return. **Follow your spirit**, wherever it might lead you. Be willing to walk down new paths and you will be presented with new opportunities. Be **forgiving**! Be **positive**! **Be loving**!

Life will be an incredibly rewarding experience. You don't want to find yourself looking back and saying, "I wish I had enjoyed life while I was living it, stopping at the yellow light instead of rushing through, letting the elderly gentlemen at the grocery store go ahead of me, or wishing I had had patience while on hold for minutes with the electric company." Life will have been good and you will have lived your life **in the present**. Above all **BE YOU!** In the end, being yourself is what really matters. Then you can say that you lived life and didn't just watch it go by without being an active participant, but that YOU really lived it, with joy, patience, gratitude, and positivity!

The 10 Be's of Positivity Path to Power Program In Ten Minutes a Day

How about incorporating the power of the 10 Be's into your daily life? Gather together with your friends and share what you've learned from each other by working with the messages in this book. It will be a worthwhile project that is also fun. Make a daily commitment for ten minutes a day to focus on one of the 10 Be's and you'll be pleased with the results.

Month 1- Read the book a few times to get a full sense of its message.

Months 2-11-Select one of the 10 Be's per month. Start a *10 Be's of Positivity Path to Power* meeting group. Meet once a month to talk about that month's focus and discuss what you might do. Choose an aspect of the 10 Be's that you are working on for that month. Jump-start your day this way by keeping a journal, and stay in touch throughout the month with group participants. When you meet each month, talk about/share ideas about what you did to focus on a particular topic at hand. You will learn from each other and will be well on your way to a path of self-empowerment.

Month 12 - Re-read the book. How did you do? I bet you will have incorporated a number of actions/ activities into your life that help you more fully embrace the person you aspire to be. This is a fun, productive and pro-active way to enjoy your life to the fullest and to share your success with others. Let me know how you do. I'd like to know.

**Coming Soon**: **The 10 Be's of Positivity for Children**

About The Author

Lynette Anneslia Turner is a Positivoligist™, certified teacher with the Robert Moss School of Active Dreaming, and certified Angelspeake™ facilitator. She was raised in Anchorage, Alaska and presently resides in Milford, Connecticut. Ms. Turner is committed to helping people embrace a path surrounded with light and love, so that they might create a more fulfilling and positive life.

An experienced Reiki practitioner, mediator, poet, personal coach, dream analysis practitioner, songwriter, musician and sound healing practitioner, Lynette believes that taking charge of your life will lead to discovery and enlightenment that can transform you. You will have the courage to move forward and effect change. It's all about B.L.I.S.S., *B*elieve *L*ife *I*s *S*omething *S*pecial, because it is, and so are you.

To offer comments on this book, to inquire about workshops for healing and happiness, listen to her inspirational and meditation CD's, or to schedule or host a 10 Be's presentation/workshop in your community, e-mail Lynette at: positivebliss1@ yahoo.com. You can write her at PO Box 762, Stratford, Connecticut 06615. View Lynette's website at www.positivebliss.com

The 10 Be's of Positivity may be purchased for use in educational, business, or sales promotions. Visit www.positivebliss.com

For information please contact:
Lynette Turner, PO Box 762, Stratford, CT 06615
positivebliss1@yahoo.com